Basic Introductions to Biology – Di
and kidney structu

ı

(A primer for Access Students and those returning to science study)

An amalgam of Basic Introductions series books 2 and 3.

By Pip Flowers

Contents

Introduction

A number of readers have commented that they would much prefer a paperback version of my 'Basic Introductions' books 2 and 3. Both these books were quite brief and therefore to make a more substantial paperback for your bookshelf I have combined these books into one for the paperback edition.

I have also taken this opportunity to tidy up some of the images and make them clearer.

I hope you enjoy the new paperback.

Types of nutrition, feeding and digestion

One of the characteristics of living things is respiration. Without cell respiration there can be no movement, no growth, no reproduction and so on. Cell respiration needs some sort of chemical input in order to release the energy for these processes. Scientists have created 2 classifications for the way this chemical input may be obtained as follows:

Autotrophs – the word means "self-feeder". Autotrophs don't need to find food and break it down. They fabricate the chemicals for cell respiration themselves. Green plants and some bacteria use solar energy to drive photosynthesis, which enables them to make carbohydrates, proteins and lipids from carbon dioxide. They are called photoautotrophs.

Other autotrophs may use chemicals-sulphur for example. These are called chemoautotrophs. They are typically highly specialised bacteria. Some exist in the layers of the earth's crust well away from the surface. Others are found in hydrothermal plumes spewing high temperature sea water (heated deep within the earth) out of vents deep down in the ocean floor.

A whole library could be put together about autotrophic nutrition, but for the rest of this book you will be studying heterotrophic nutrition.

Heterotrophs - Heterotrophs need to obtain food and digest it. There are various methods used by different organisms. Briefly the types can be summarised as:

1. **Holozoic**- most free-living animals. Food is taken in and broken down/digested internally. This can be solid food or in liquid form (e.g. aphids feed on sap). There is a wide range of feeding strategies in this group.

2. **Saprobiontic (saprotrophic)** – These secrete enzymes and digest externally, then absorb the broken down nutrients. Examples are fungi or decomposing species of bacteria
3. **Mutualist** – An association exists between two organisms from which both gain some benefit
4. **Parasitic** – an organism lives in or on another and obtains nutrition from it.

In this book you will be getting to grips with holozoic nutrition- with special emphasis on human nutrition and digestion.

Holozoic Digestion – the processes

Many years ago, scientists started to describe five components of holozoic nutrition. Scientist loved to file things into neat pigeonholes in those days. Many still do!

Component 1 – Ingestion. The taking in of food.

Component 2 – Digestion. The progressive mechanical and/or chemical breakdown of the ingested food into molecules small enough to pass across the gut lining.

Component 3 – Absorption. Taking up the small molecules resulting from digestion into the bloodstream.

Component 4 – Assimilation. The use made by the body of the absorbed nutrients.

Component 5 – Egestion. Where the body gets rid of undigested food wastes.

These headings are a useful way of understanding how an organism extracts useful substances from food for their own purposes. However, beware of thinking of them as isolated stages. Ingestion does take place in the mouth and egestion by the anus via the large intestine. However, other components happen in a multitude of places, often simultaneously. For instance in the mouth there are ingestion, digestion *and* absorption processes taking place.

Children often describe the tummy as the seat of digestion. Older students will say digestion also happens in the mouth and small intestine. More advanced biology students refine this to include the mouth, stomach, duodenum and large intestine, and so on. Even this is an over simplification.

There are many permutations for the way these basic processes occur in holozoic digestion. In this book you are predominantly studying digestion in humans..... specifically modern humans as homo sapiens.

Modern humans are omnivorous. We have plant and animal matter in our diets. Early bipeds (e.g. the Australopithecines who lived between one and five million years ago) had a mainly-possibly solely- herbivorous diet. Plant matter is rough, tough, unrewarding stuff to eat. You need a big, specialised digestive system to wring the maximum nourishment out of it. Study of Australopithecine remains suggests that at least some of them had a much larger digestive system to cope with a high plant diet.

This diversity is present today. Herbivores tackle digestion in various ways. Cattle for instance digest in two passes. Firstly they swallow the food and it undergoes some breakdown by resident bacteria in the animal's gut. Then the food is returned to the mouth for further mechanical breakdown (chewing the cud), after which it is swallowed and broken down further by the cow's digestive enzymes. Even then there is still a lot of waste produced - try walking across a cow field in your best shoes!

Rabbits do it differently-they don't chew the cud after bacterial digestion. They egest it and then eat the egested waste (poo) for digestion by their own enzymes. Owls (carnivores) have a fascinating way of digesting food. There's lots of information on the internet if you are interested.

Although it is a subject of ongoing debate, many evolutionary biologists feel that the switch to a higher protein diet in human evolution is linked to increased brain size. Maybe having a smaller digestive system reduces the energy needed to actually digest the food, meaning the saved energy can go into brain development instead. There are other possibilities. Again, if you are interested, follow the debate on the internet. Or specialise in evolution at university.

This diagram summarises these examples of the variations in holozoic nutrition.

A comparison of three variations in holozoic nutrition

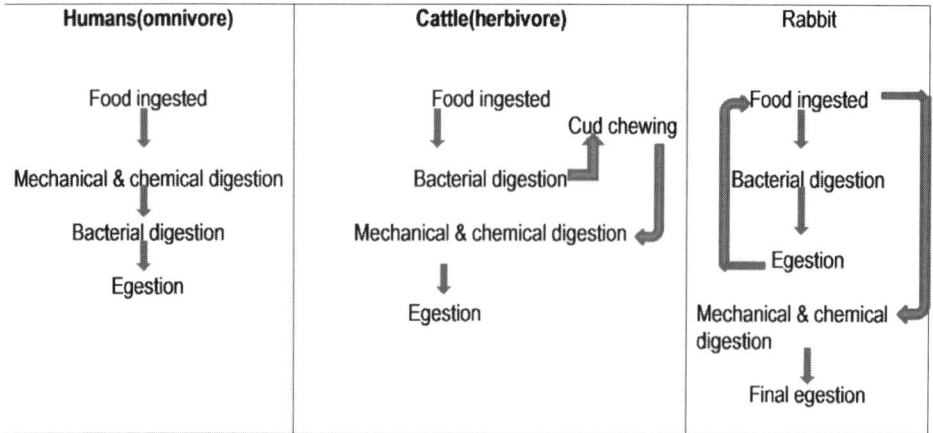

Humans(omnivore)	Cattle(herbivore)	Rabbit
Food ingested ↓ Mechanical & chemical digestion ↓ Bacterial digestion ↓ Egestion	Food ingested ↓ Cud chewing Bacterial digestion ↑ Mechanical & chemical digestion ↓ Egestion	Food ingested ↓ Bacterial digestion ↓ Egestion Mechanical & chemical digestion ↓ Final egestion

Digestion – what do mechanical and chemical mean?

Mechanical breakdown of the food taken in is obviously accomplished by chewing. However mechanical pressure also happens further along the digestive tract- to some extent in humans but in other species it is very significant in breakdown of food.

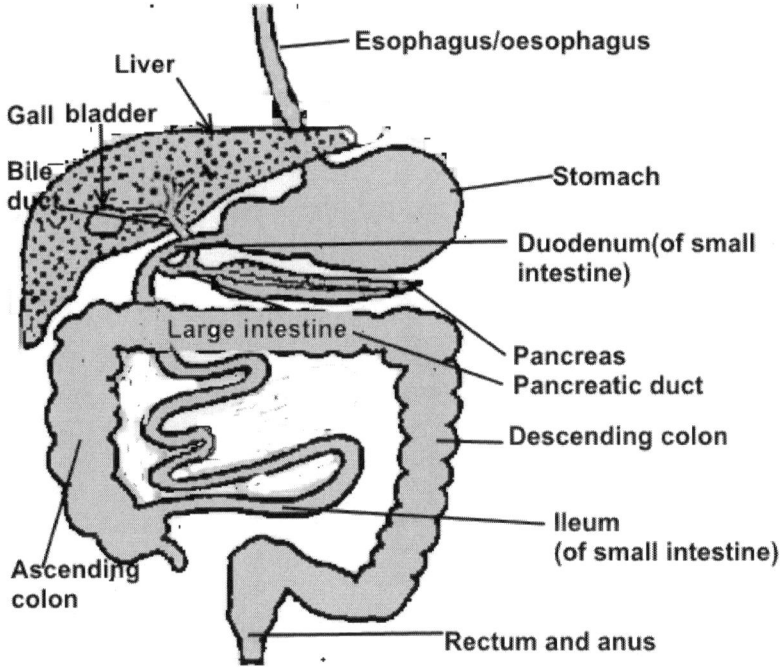

There are three layers of muscle in the stomach which churn and mix the food; in the large intestine haustral churning is also a potent force. In birds the swallowed food may be stored in a holding chamber called the crop, before being passed to the stomach, which has a specialised chamber called the gizzard or gastric mill. If you've ever wondered why some birds peck up grit, here's your answer. The grit and stones go into the gizzard, and help mash up the food ready for chemical digestion. It is not only birds that have a gizzard- earthworms do too!

Chemical breakdown

In the first book of the series, (Basic Introductions to Biology-Cells, tissues and circulation) you may recall reading about enzymes. Here is a condensed extract from that book.

You have already discovered that enzymes are globular proteins. Enzymes are the reason we are alive! Each body process involves enzymes to ensure it happens smoothly. Enzymes make it easier for chemical reactions to occur without being used up themselves. Enzymes may speed up the breaking down of substances (catabolic reactions-e.g. the digestion of polysaccharides into simpler sugars by the enzyme amylase), or the anabolic building up of substances (e.g. DNA from individual nucleotides by DNA polymerase).

It has been known for many years that these globular proteins have a specialised area called the "active site". The shape of this active site is complementary to the particular substance(s) that enzyme catalyses. The substance an enzyme causes to react is called the substrate. It was recognised that specific enzymes seemed to work with specific substrates. So, pepsin (a protein digesting enzyme) never worked with starch (a carbohydrate).

It's also been known that somehow when the active site of enzyme binds with its similarly shaped substrate, either the substrate breaks down (catabolic) or is added to (anabolic).

For years this was known as the 'lock and key' model. The diagram below shows the basic idea of an exact match between enzyme and substrate.

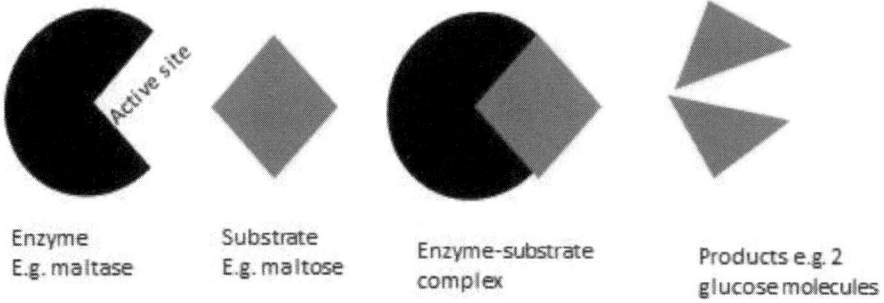

Enzyme
E.g. maltase

Substrate
E.g. maltose

Enzyme-substrate complex

Products e.g. 2 glucose molecules

A few years ago it became obvious that this very rigid model didn't match reality, so now the model is that of an induced fit. The theory is that enzyme and substrate bind loosely but then the enzyme protein deforms to fit tightly round the substrate and exerts force on it causing the catabolic/anabolic reaction to take place more easily.

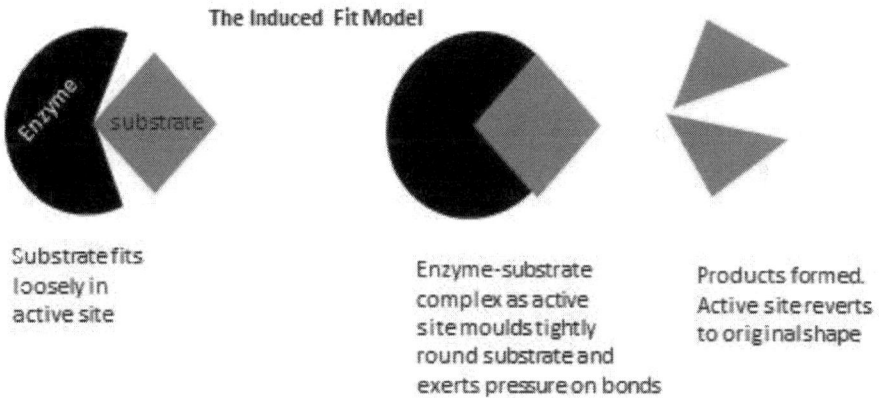

The Induced Fit Model

Substrate fits loosely in active site

Enzyme-substrate complex as active site moulds tightly round substrate and exerts pressure on bonds

Products formed. Active site reverts to original shape

This has led to the suggestion that while some enzymes are very specific- others are less so and due to induced fit can adjust to a range of reasonably similar shaped substrates. Science moves on.

Note also that being proteins, enzymes are affected by pH and temperature.

Digestion-carbohydrate breakdown

You may recall from Book 1 in the Basic Introductions series that carbohydrates range from simple sugars with just one sugar unit, through more complex carbohydrates with two sugar units (disaccharides) right up to giant carbohydrates called polysaccharides with many sugar units.

Here is a reminder of some examples:

Monosaccharide	Disaccharide	Polysaccharide
Glucose	Sucrose	Starch(plants)
Fructose	Maltose	Glycogen (animals)
Galactose	Lactose	Cellulose
Ribose		

The polysaccharides and disaccharides may comprise a mixture of simple sugars, for example:-

Making disaccharides

GLUCOSE - GLUCOSE →MALTOSE

GLUCOSE - FRUCTOSE→ SUCROSE

GLUCOSE - GALACTOSE→LACTOSE

Monosaccharides are a single molecule and therefore do not need breaking down in the digestive tract. They can be absorbed into the bloodstream as they are. In fact they can be absorbed in the mouth by simple diffusion into the bloodstream. This is possible because the cells lining the mouth are very thin squamous cells, which you met several times in Book 1.

Squamous epithelium

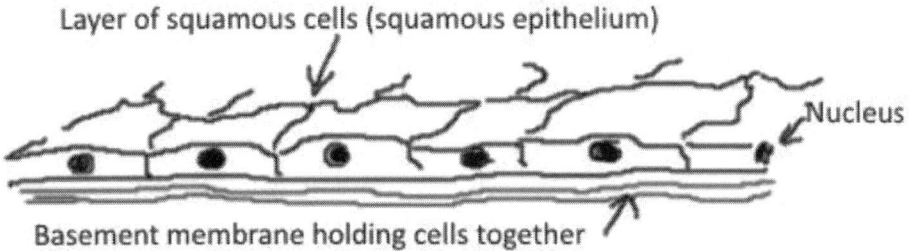

Layer of squamous cells (squamous epithelium)

Nucleus

Basement membrane holding cells together

However most of the carbohydrate we eat is in more complex form; disaccharides, oligosaccharides (between three and nine simple sugars) or polysaccharides such as starch from plants. All of these need digesting – breaking down into monosaccharides if the body is to use them.

When we ingest food there is a reflex action of chewing. The salivary glands are also stimulated to release a cocktail of water, mucus and a carbohydrate digesting enzyme called salivary amylase. The enzyme works well in the neutral pH conditions in the mouth, and readily breaks down some of the starch – but not completely. The end product of starch digestion in the mouth is the disaccharide maltose. This will require further breakdown to glucose later in the duodenum.

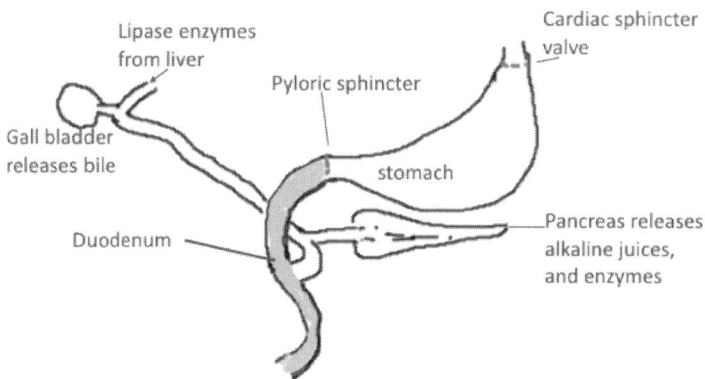

The duodenum is the first, very short (about 20-25cm) length of the small intestine. It is here that the majority of enzyme controlled digestion is completed. In the above sketch, notice that it is carrying liquefied food (called chyme) from the highly acid stomach. It also has a duct bringing substances from the liver, gall bladder and pancreas.

When carbohydrate enters the duodenum from the stomach, fluids from the pancreas stabilise the pH back to neutral (7.0), and also bring carbohydrate digesting enzymes (e.g. pancreatic amylase (which continue chopping polysaccharides up. The cells in the wall of the duodenum also release enzymes (e.g. sucrase, maltase etc.)and this battery of enzymes complete the breakdown of a lot of the carbohydrates into monosaccharides (see the previous table).

However some carbohydrates are "resistant starch" or "fibre", which remains intact despite the enzymes. These carbohydrates will be further attacked by our resident bacteria in the large intestine (note the similarity with herbivores). The breakdown products of bacterial digestion in the large intestine have been found to be very beneficial. Some contain substances called glucosinolates. Research suggests that glucosinolates inhibit development of cancers. Bacterial digestion also liberates vitamins which are absorbed into the bloodstream across the walls of the large intestine.

.

Digestion-carbohydrate uptake

Carbohydrate uptake happens in the jejunum and the ileum. The inside of the small intestine has wrinkles or infolding called villi. Villi increase the surface area; the intestine is only about 2.5cm in diameter. However if you stretched it widthways so the infoldings lay flat it would be much bigger. You can see that the cells making up a villus have microvilli (see Book 1), enhancing the effect further.

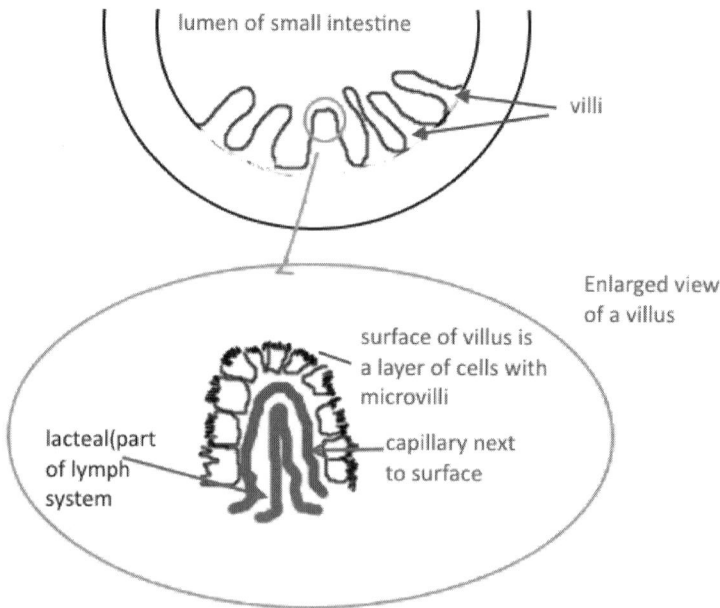

The process of carbohydrate uptake frim the ileum happens like this:

1. Sodium is pumped out of the cells lining the ileum and into the bloodstream by active transport.
2. This leaves the inside of the cells lower in sodium than the digested food in the intestine.

3. Therefore sodium diffuses from the food into the cells, high to low concentration.
4. The sodium "co-transports" glucose and amino acids into the cell with it.
5. The inside of the cell becomes higher in glucose and amino acids than the bloodstream, and they move by facilitated diffusion into the blood. (to be carried away to the liver via the hepatic portal vein).
6. The high glucose levels in the cells also create an osmotic gradient, causing water to move from food into cells and from the cells into the bloodstream.

The diagram summarises the process. Read it from left to right.

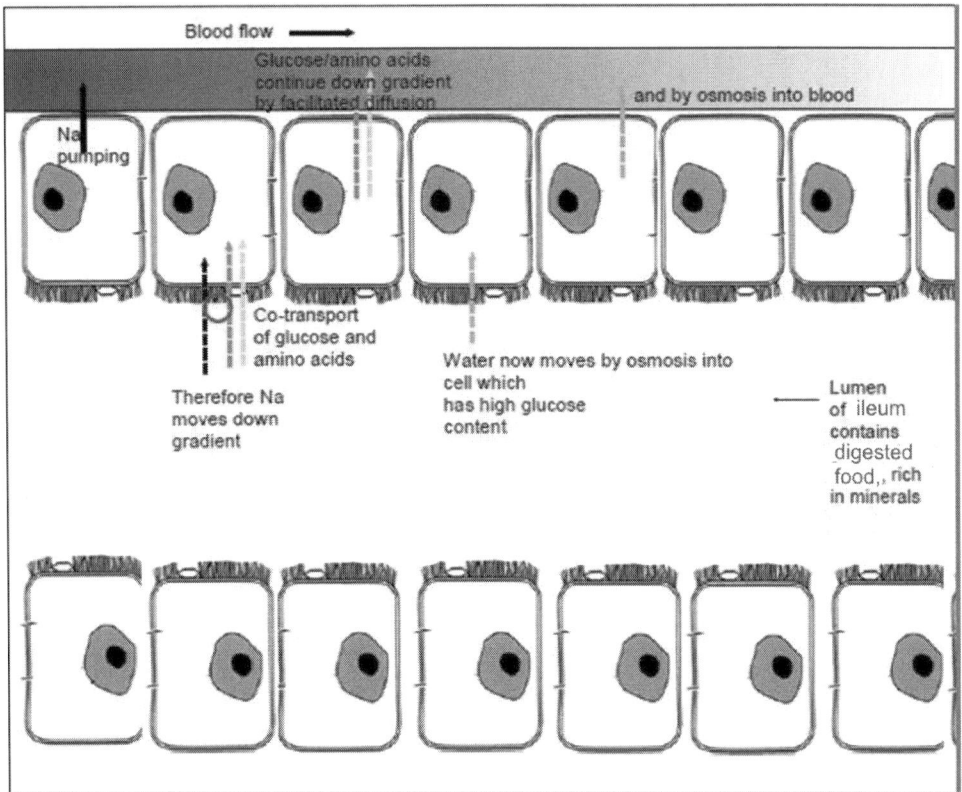

Blood flow

Glucose/amino acids continue down gradient by facilitated diffusion

and by osmosis into blood

Na pumping

Co-transport of glucose and amino acids

Therefore Na moves down gradient

Water now moves by osmosis into cell which has high glucose content

Lumen of ileum contains digested food,, rich in minerals

Digestion-protein breakdown and uptake of amino acids

You may recall from Book 1 that proteins consist of large numbers of amino acids joined together. Digestion therefore will have to break the peptide bonds holding the amino acids together, in order that they can be absorbed into the bloodstream in the small intestine.

As with carbohydrates, protein digestion is a two stage process.

Stage 1 – Protein digestion begins in the stomach. Eating stimulate the release of hydrochloric acid from specialised cells in the stomach wall. This creates a very acid (as acid as pH 1.5-2.0) environment. You will recall from Book 1 that proteins become denatured when exposed to extremes of pH. However the acid conditions also lead to the activation of pepsinogen into the protease enzyme pepsin.

The pepsin begins the protein breakdown process, but the result is to produce protein fragments containing several amino acids. In due course these are released through the pyloric sphincter valve into the duodenum.

Stage 2 - Pancreatic protease enzymes flow via the pancreatic duct into the duodenum. They are in the pancreatic juices which also stabilise the pH to neutral-ish. Most other enzymes will not work at the stomach pH. There are a number of these and they complete the final breakdown of protein to individual amino acids.

Uptake of the amino acids happens alongside the uptake of monosaccharides. See the diagram and explanation in the previous section.

Digestion-lipid breakdown and uptake of fatty acids

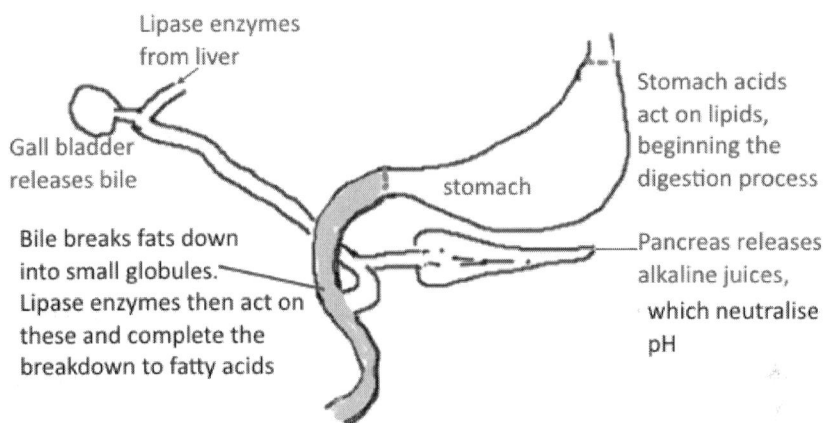

Lipase enzymes
from liver

Stomach acids
act on lipids,
beginning the
digestion process

Gall bladder
releases bile

stomach

Bile breaks fats down
into small globules.
Lipase enzymes then act on
these and complete the
breakdown to fatty acids

Pancreas releases
alkaline juices,
which neutralise
pH

Again we have a multi-stage process. In the stomach, the conditions have a weakening effect on lipid structure. However the stomach activity also directly triggers the release of bile and lipase enzymes into the duodenum (see the above diagram). You can also see a description of the two stage digestion in the diagram.

In the description of monosaccharide and amino acid uptake there was no mention of fatty acids. These are absorbed in a different way.

Key points for the uptake of fatty acids

Short chain fatty acids	Larger fatty acids
These diffuse directly into the hepatic portal vein, which carries them to the liver.	1. These enter the epithelial cells of the small intestine. 2. Where the smooth endoplasmic reticulum and Golgi body converts them into larger molecules called

	chylomicrons.
	3. Chylomicrons are taken up by branches of the lymph system called lacteals.
	4. They then travel through the lymph system and eventually rejoin the circulatory system via the subclavian veins in the thoracic region.

Digestion – regulation and control

A very complex set of responses and triggers involving hormones, the brains and nerves is involved in controlling feeding and digestion.

Before eating

Reduced fat intake and fat levels results in reduced levels of the hormone **leptin** being released into the bloodstream. As the stomach becomes empty, specialised cells in the stomach wall release increased quantities of the hormone **ghrelin** into the bloodstream. An area of the brain called the **hypothalamus** detects these changes in the blood. One of the many functions of the hypothalamus is monitoring and responding to the need for food. Leptin has an inhibitory effect on appetite, so reducing levels makes us feel hungry. Ghrelin is an appetite hormone; as levels of ghrelin rise, we feel hungrier and hungrier.

Incidentally, introducing the leptin gene into food crops can minimise pest damage. The pests take a nibble then feel full!

The following diagram "Before eating" summarises these changes.

Before eating

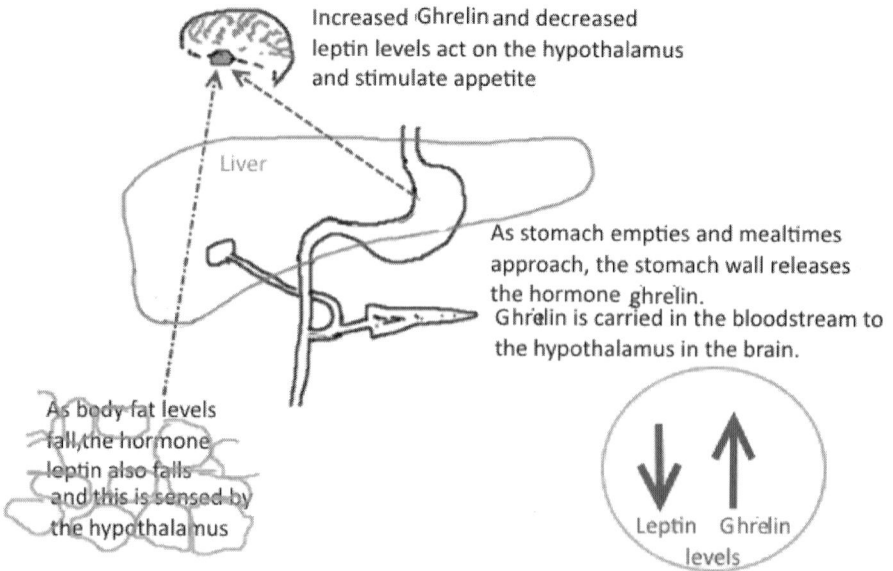

Increased Ghrelin and decreased leptin levels act on the hypothalamus and stimulate appetite

Liver

As stomach empties and mealtimes approach, the stomach wall releases the hormone ghrelin.
Ghrelin is carried in the bloodstream to the hypothalamus in the brain.

As body fat levels fall, the hormone leptin also falls and this is sensed by the hypothalamus

Leptin   Ghrelin
levels

While eating

Ingestion of feed sends nerve signals to G cells in the stomach wall, triggering them to release the hormone **gastrin**. Gastrin is an endocrine hormone. Endocrine hormones are always released into the bloodstream. This stimulates various glands in the stomach wall to secrete hydrochloric acid and also pepsinogen, which becomes converted to active pepsin by the acid.

The digestion of food in the stomach sends nerve signals to sets of specialised cells in the duodenum wall, which begin to secrete hormones. Examples of these substances are:

CCK (cholecystokinin) - this hormone causes the gall bladder to squeeze stored bile into the duodenum. It also stimulates the pancreas to release its enzymes in its role as an exocrine gland. Exocrine glands secrete their products into ducts or cavities (contrast this with endocrine glands). In older books you may see CCK named pancreozymin.

Secretin – has several roles including inducing the pancreas to release vital alkaline juices. These restore the highly acid chyme from the stomach to a neutral state. Failure to do this would prevent the duodenal enzymes being able to work.

Incretins- these hormones carry early warning to the pancreas and trigger specialised beta (β) cells to start releasing the hormone insulin ahead of blood glucose levels rising. It has been found that insulin can have an inhibitory effect on appetite above threshold levels.

The diagram summarises these changes.

As feeding begins and food enters the duodenum

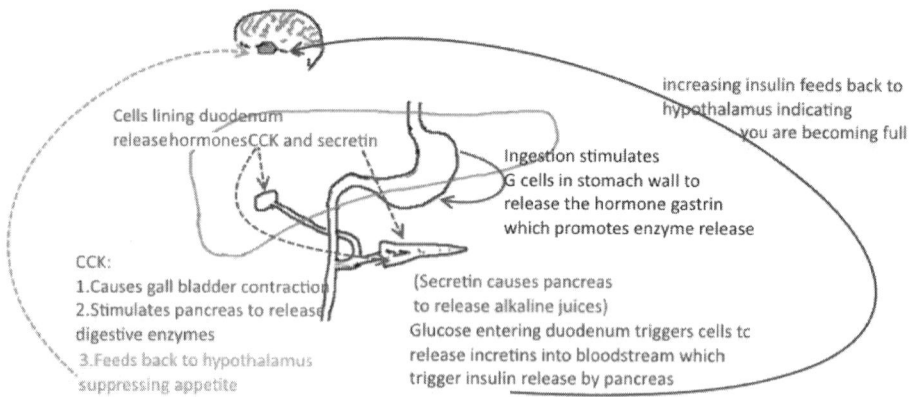

Cells lining duodenum release hormones CCK and secretin

increasing insulin feeds back to hypothalamus indicating you are becoming full

Ingestion stimulates G cells in stomach wall to release the hormone gastrin which promotes enzyme release

CCK:
1. Causes gall bladder contraction
2. Stimulates pancreas to release digestive enzymes
3. Feeds back to hypothalamus suppressing appetite

(Secretin causes pancreas to release alkaline juices)
Glucose entering duodenum triggers cells to release incretins into bloodstream which trigger insulin release by pancreas

As we become full

Stretch receptors in the stomach send nerve signals resulting in reduced ghrelin levels. The increase fat levels result in a surge in leptin in the bloodstream, while blood insulin levels reach a high, Furthermore, cells in the small intestine release a further substance called PYY into the bloodstream. The hypothalamus detects these shifts and effectively signals that satiety (fullness) has been reached.

You can readily appreciate that if the receptors in the hypothalamus (or elsewhere) lose their sensitivity to the various hormones, there can be profound effects on health. For example obesity – the feeling of fullness will not be reached when it should.

The final diagram illustrates these changes.

As body reaches sufficiency

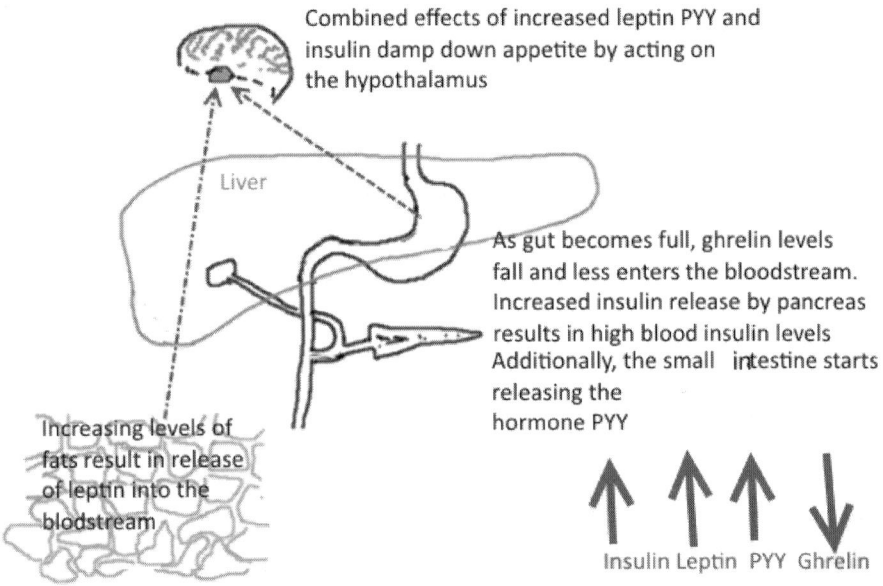

Combined effects of increased leptin PYY and insulin damp down appetite by acting on the hypothalamus

Liver

As gut becomes full, ghrelin levels fall and less enters the bloodstream. Increased insulin release by pancreas results in high blood insulin levels Additionally, the small intestine starts releasing the hormone PYY

Increasing levels of fats result in release of leptin into the blodstream

Insulin Leptin PYY Ghrelin

Our increasing understanding of these processes has facilitated the development of many new medications blocking or enhancing these feedback pathways in diseases such as diabetes and also increasingly, obesity.

Homeostasis – blood sugar regulation

After the absorption of carbohydrate, the monosaccharides pass into the hepatic portal vein and are carried to the liver.

Location of the hepatic portal vein

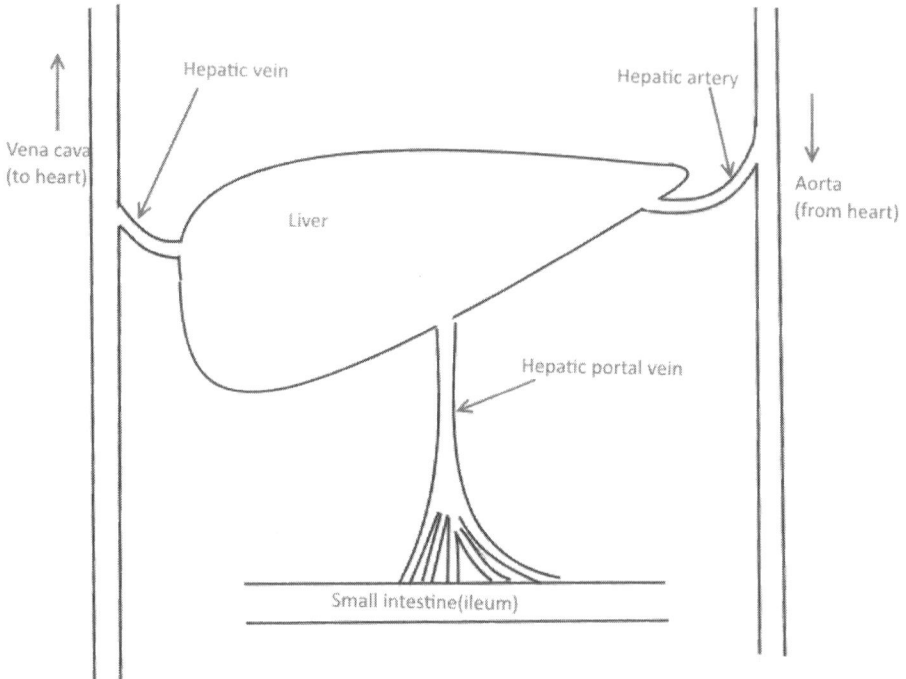

The increasing levels of blood sugar are detected by cells in the pancreas. The beta (β) cells of the pancreas respond by releasing the hormone insulin into the bloodstream. Insulin binds to (amongst others) liver and muscle cells, increasing their rate of uptake of glucose from the blood passing through the tissues.

Depending on the amount in the bloodstream, this glucose will be converted to the storage carbohydrate glycogen for future use. It is safer to store the glucose thus, as it avoids the osmotic problems that would arise if cells contained high quantities of glucose. Once the glycogen stores become full, any surplus glucose taken up is converted to fat and stored in fat cells around the body.

When blood sugar levels fall below normal, a different set of pancreatic cells called alpha (α) cells release a different hormone called glucagon.

Glucagon causes blood glucose levels to be topped up by the breakdown of glycogen back to glucose, which is then released into the bloodstream. Whereas the insulin mediated glucose to glycogen conversion takes place in liver and muscle cells, the glucagon mediated glycogen (and fat) conversion to glucose only occurs in the liver.

Homeostasis works by a system of negative feedback; any movement away from the normal or desired level triggers a body response back towards normal. You will often see diagrams of the following type to show what is happening.

Blood sugar regulation

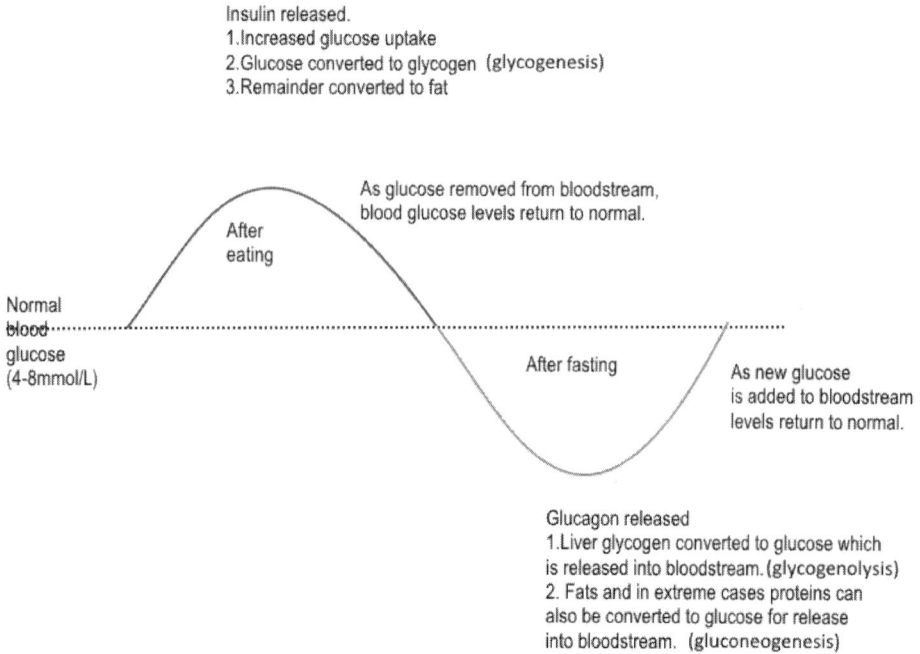

Insulin released.
1. Increased glucose uptake
2. Glucose converted to glycogen (glycogenesis)
3. Remainder converted to fat

As glucose removed from bloodstream, blood glucose levels return to normal.

After eating

Normal blood glucose (4-8mmol/L)

After fasting

As new glucose is added to bloodstream levels return to normal.

Glucagon released
1. Liver glycogen converted to glucose which is released into bloodstream. (glycogenolysis)
2. Fats and in extreme cases proteins can also be converted to glucose for release into bloodstream. (gluconeogenesis)

While these diagrams are useful, it is important to realise that both insulin and glucagon are constantly being secreted under average conditions. Rather than turning glucagon off and insulin on when we eat, the body just fine tunes by turning insulin secretion up and glucagon down. This enables a smooth but very fast response without sharp peaks and troughs.

Blood sugar regulation and diabetes

Not all forms of diabetes relate to problems in blood sugar regulation.

Type 1 diabetes - The type 1 sufferer releases insufficient or no insulin. This is because their pancreatic beta cells have been damaged or destroyed. This could be due to an infection, chemicals or an auto-immune response (where the body's immune system turns on the sufferer). They have lost the negative feedback effect and blood sugar is effectively unregulated and climbs much higher than normal(hyperglycaemia).

Up to the renal threshold, the **type 1** subject can excrete excess glucose in the urine. Above this the situation deteriorates. The short term results can be serious and lead to a diabetic coma and death. Longer term with inadequate or no treatment, ongoing damage affects vision, heart and body mass. Energy levels are low. Treatment revolves around enabling the sufferer to self-administer insulin. In most cases this is by injection. Type 1 diabetes used to be called "juvenile onset diabetes" but is commonly referred to now as "insulin dependent diabetes".

Type 2 (II) diabetes – Formerly called "mature onset diabetes" it is now known as "non-insulin dependent diabetes" (NIDD). Again the sufferer has difficulty keeping blood sugar levels down to normal. However this time they may well be producing enough insulin. The problem is one of insulin resistance in liver and muscle cells. The cells do not respond to insulin by increasing glucose uptake from the blood. Again, the effects can be serious. Traditional treatment revolved around self-management of diet.

Diabetes Insipidus – the term "diabetes" actually means "excess urination". Types 1 and 2 diabetes are "sugar diabetes" or diabetes mellitus. Diabetes insipidus results in excess urination for a different reason. Commonly due to an injury to the head, a knock or blow may damage the hypothalamus or pituitary gland. These are both important in regulation of water levels. In diabetes insipidus, the subject does not produce enough of the hormone ADH (anti-diuretic hormone) which helps water retention.

Diabetes drugs – biochemistry

Diabetes pharmacology is an area of huge and exciting development. The following information shows just a few of the approaches currently available. New drugs are constantly under development.

Insulin options

Oral insulin would get broken down in the stomach before it reached the site of absorption in the ileum. For most people self-injection is the preferred method of treatment-in some cases n automated mini-pump can be used. Available in three formulations, designed to match the diabetic's requirements at different times of day. The types are, fast acting, slow acting and intermediate acting. You would not want to take fast acting at bed time due to the danger of a hypoglycaemic attack while asleep, when blood sugar falls dangerously low.

Insulin Lispro is a popular rapid acting, shorter lasting insulin. It can be injected immediately before eating

Insulin glargine - is injected but then forms microscopic crystalline layers in the fat, dissolving slowly over the next several hours

Clinical insulin is produced by biotechnology.

DPP-4 inhibitors

Incretins activate B cells to produce insulin. However to avoid runaway insulin production, enzymes are present in the pancreas that inactivate incretins. One such enzyme is called DPP-4(dipeptidyl peptidase-4). By inhibiting DPP-4, diabetes drugs such as gliptins enhance the amount of insulin being released which can benefit Type 1 sufferers.

Acarbose

Acarbose inhibits enzymes which break down starch and glycogen (alpha glucosidase
enzymes)

This slows down the absorption of starchy foods from the intestine. Acarbose could therefore be beneficial to Types 1 or 2 subjects.

Actos and Competact

These drugs increase the sensitivity of insulin receptors in liver, fat and muscle cells. They are beneficial to Type 2 sufferers.

Biguanides

One of the most prescribed drugs for diabetes (and other conditions) is **Metformin.** Research has revealed that Type 2 sufferers typically have three times the normal rate of gluconeogenesis (boosting blood sugar through fat and protein breakdown). Metformin suppresses gluconeogenesis. **Eucreas** is a combination of Metformin and a DPP4 inhibitor.

Pramlintides – Symlin

This is not currently available on prescription in the UK. The medication mimics a naturally occurring hormone and is claimed to inhibit glucagon release, slow down stomach emptying and also send satiety signals to the brain.

There have been reports of a heightened risk of serious hypoglycaemia.

The kidneys – basic structure

We have a pair of kidneys-they are found in the small of the back.

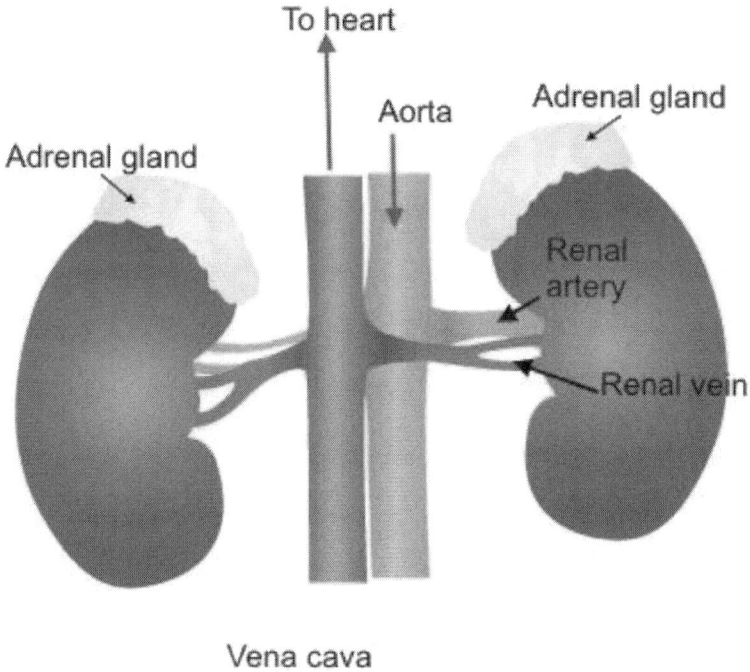

If a student dissects a fresh kidney and takes a (rather iffy camera phone) photo, this is about all that is visible.

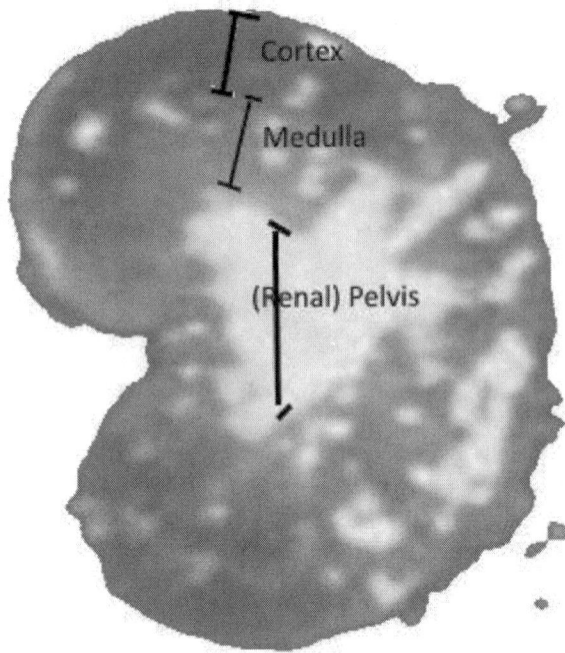

Three distinct layers, the cortex (outer layer), medulla (middle layer) and the renal pelvis (the innermost white layer). With a bit of imagination you can make out the fairly tough outer renal capsule holding the structure together.

Kidneys contain millions of tiny filtration units called nephrons. The following diagram shows the layout of a kidney along with a representation of a nephron.

Outline drawing of gross kidney structure showing typical location of a nephron

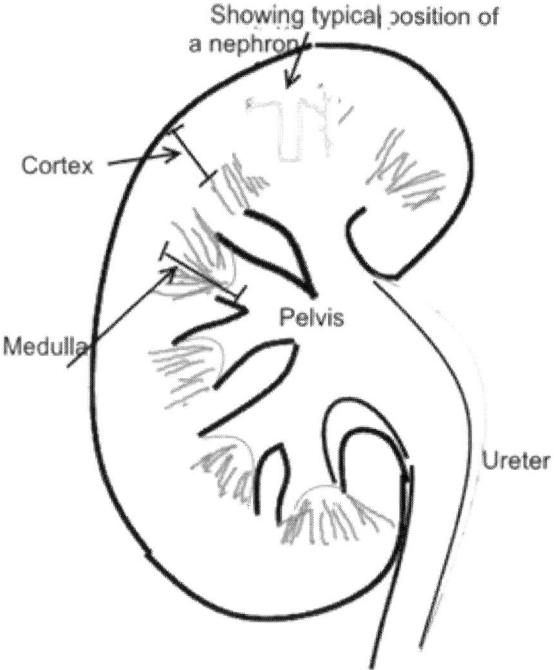

Showing typical position of a nephron

Cortex

Medulla

Pelvis

Ureter

Basic nephron structure

The diagram shows the basic structure of a single nephron in a human.

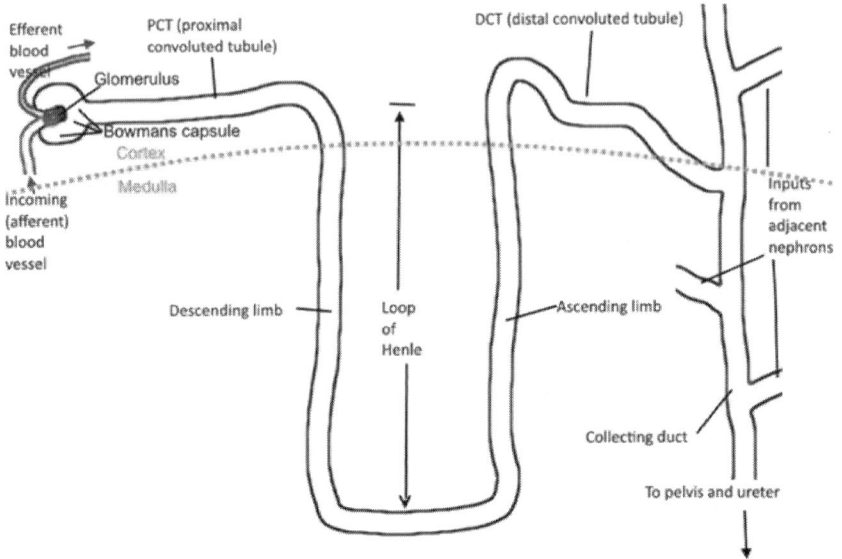

The majority of nephrons have the Bowmans Capsule and Glomerulus in the outermost layer (the cortex). The glomerulus is a network of blood vessels packed into the cup of the Bowmans Capsule. The afferent blood vessel carries blood into the glomerulus from the renal artery. The efferent blood vessel carries blood away from the glomerulus to the renal vein.

Detailed view of the Bowmans Capsule and Glomerulus

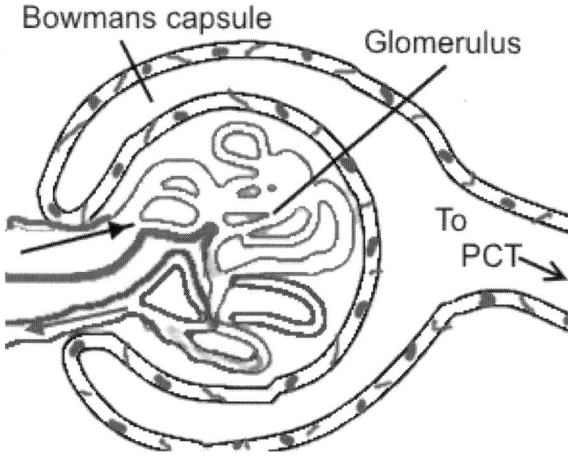

Notice how much wider the afferent (incoming) blood vessel is than the outgoing. You can also see that the Bowmans Capsule is actually formed from a single layer of squamous epithelium cells. You might recall these thin flat cells from Book 1. The blood vessels form a dense network called a **rete**. In some textbooks you will see the whole structure, Bowmans Capsule and Glomerulus referred to as the **Malpighian Body**.

The Loop of Henle is predominantly in the medullary region while the Proximal Convoluted Tubule and Distal Convoluted Tubule are in the cortex.

Notice that the nephron (and others) discharges into a larger **collecting duct.** This duct carries the urine to the renal pelvis and from thence via the ureters to the bladder. The rest is history.

Urine – where does it come from?

In Book 2 which dealt with digestion, the breakdown of proteins into amino acids was described. Amino acids travel in the hepatic portal vein to the liver for processing. Book 1 describes the chemical structure of proteins.

Liver cells start to break down the amino acids. In doing so the nitrogenous group is released and this promptly forms toxic ammonia through a chemical reaction.

Liver cells are equipped to deal with this and quickly process the ammonia through a series of reactions called the Ornithine (or Urea) Cycle. The ammonia is converted into a much safer substance, urea. Combined with water, urea gives rise to urine.

The urea is now carried away from the liver in the bloodstream. About a minute later the urea arrives at the kidneys.

Incidentally, the liver cells can make use of the carbon, hydrogen and oxygen resulting from amino acid breakdown.

Nephron processes- (1) Ultrafiltration

Summary

Ultrafiltration is the first nephron process. Ultrafiltration filters the blood.

How it happens

The difference in diameters (and therefore flow capacity) of the afferent and efferent blood vessels results in a back pressure developing in the glomerulus.

The walls of the glomerular blood vessels are a specialised type of fenestrated capillary and the walls of the Bowmans capsule are permeable to small molecules. The back pressure therefore forces small molecules out of the bloodstream through these narrow gaps into the nephron, towards the PCT. This process is called **ultrafiltration**.

Bowmans capsule

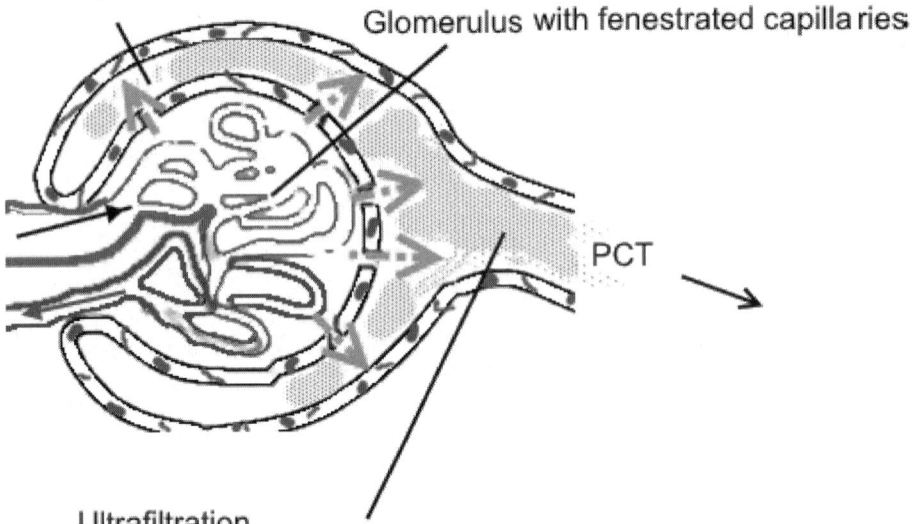

Glomerulus with fenestrated capillaries

PCT

Ultrafiltration
Increased pressure within the glomerulus
forces small molecules out of the bloodstream
into the nephron. Examples include:
*Water
*Ions(eg sodium,potassium,chloride etc)
*Glucose
*Amino acids
*Urea
*Creatinine

A fenestrated capillary.

The dots represent holes in the squamous cells making up
the glomerular capillaries.

Ultrafiltration is very effective at pressure filtering the small molecules out of the blood and into the nephron. The resulting liquid is called the **glomerular filtrate**. However the diagram shows that the majority of these substances are needed by the body. For example glucose, ions and amino acids, which have just been obtained through digestion. (Digestion is detailed in Book 2)

The processes of reclaiming the valuable substances, while letting the wastes (e.g. urea) go must be carried out very quickly, to avoid losing them in the urine. The next section describes the first of these processes.

Nephron processes (2) – Selective reabsorption (obligate)

In the PCT vital substances including glucose, amino acids and water are reabsorbed back into the bloodstream. This process happens in a similar way to carbohydrate uptake in the ileum (detailed in the digestion section). Check back to Book 1 if you need to refresh your understanding of active transport, diffusion, facilitated diffusion and osmosis.

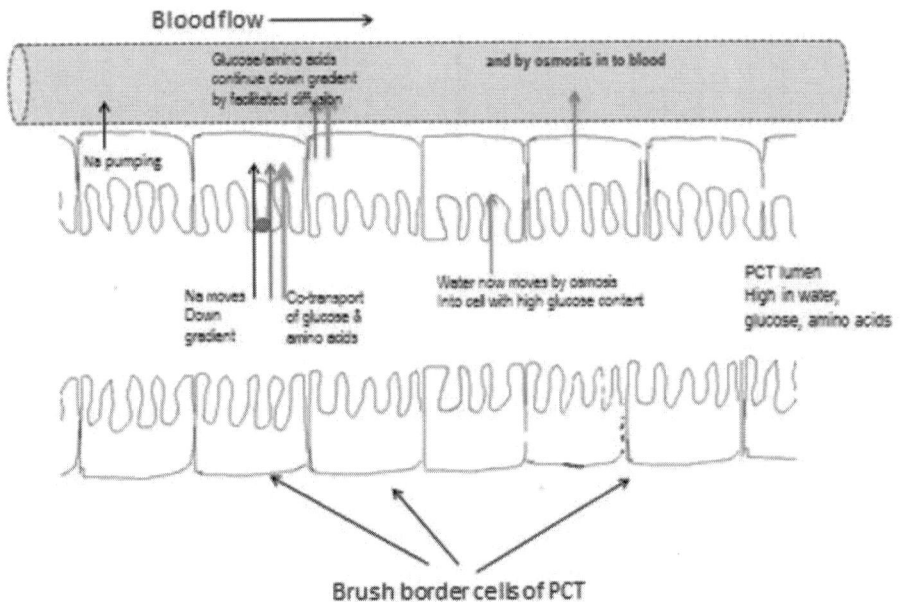

Blood flow ⟶

Glucose/amino acids continue down gradient by facilitated diffusion

and by osmosis in to blood

Na pumping

Na moves Down gradient

Co-transport of glucose & amino acids

Water now moves by osmosis Into cell with high glucose content

PCT lumen High in water, glucose, amino acids

Brush border cells of PCT

How it happens

1. Sodium is actively pumped from brush border cells lining the PCT into the bloodstream.

2. This increases the sodium content of the blood.
3. Consequently, sodium diffuses into the brush border cell <u>down the concentration gradient</u> from the (high sodium) glomerular filtrate.
4. The movement of sodium co-transports glucose and amino acids into the cell with it. This is due to special transport proteins on the microvilli. (Known as a glucose symporter).
5. The brush border cell thus becomes higher in glucose and amino acids than the blood.
6. Therefore glucose and amino acids move into the blood by (facilitated) diffusion.
7. The high glucose content of the cells also causes water to move into the cells and from thence into the bloodstream by osmosis.

This reabsorption happens at a pretty constant rate. It does account for reabsorption of a very high percentage of the water in the glomerular filtrate as well as all of the glucose and amino acids. However there is no fine tuning when we are under or over hydrated.

Note that the reabsorption of water means that the concentration of substances (e.g. urea) remaining in the nephron must increase. They are now in a smaller volume of water.

Nephron processes (3) – Water reabsorption in the Loop of Henle (obligate)

In the Loop of Henle further water is reabsorbed from the nephron into the bloodstream. This is aided by differences in water permeability in the descending and ascending limbs.

How it happens

The descending limb of the Loop of Henle is water permeable, whereas the ascending limb is water impermeable.

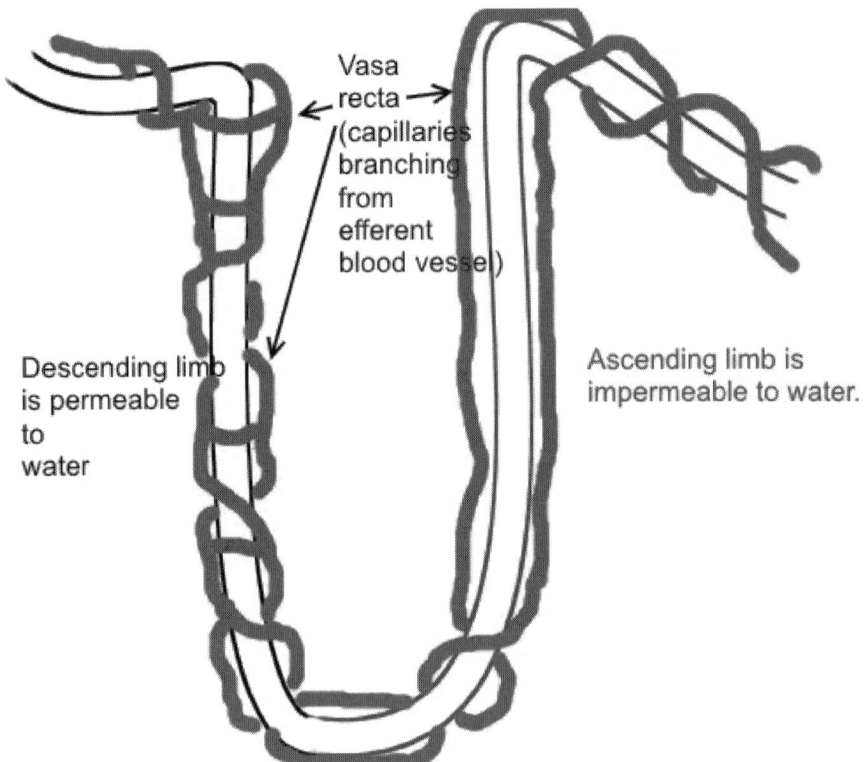

Vasa recta (capillaries branching from efferent blood vessel)

Descending limb is permeable to water

Ascending limb is impermeable to water.

The blood supply from the efferent arteriole divides and sub-divides to form a network of blood vessels called the vasa recta as shown in the diagram. These lie close to the nephron tubules, allowing ready movement of substances between nephron contents and the bloodstream – and vice versa.

The walls of the descending limb of the Loop of Henle are water permeable, whereas the ascending limb is water impermeable.

Yet again a series of processes is first driven by active transport. This time sodium and chloride ions are actively pumped out of the ascending limb into the medullary tissue.

This leads to a high solute concentration in the medulla, drawing water out of the descending limb by osmosis. The water then continues into the bloodstream.

The sodium and chloride ions diffuse into the descending limb. The following diagram summarises the processes.

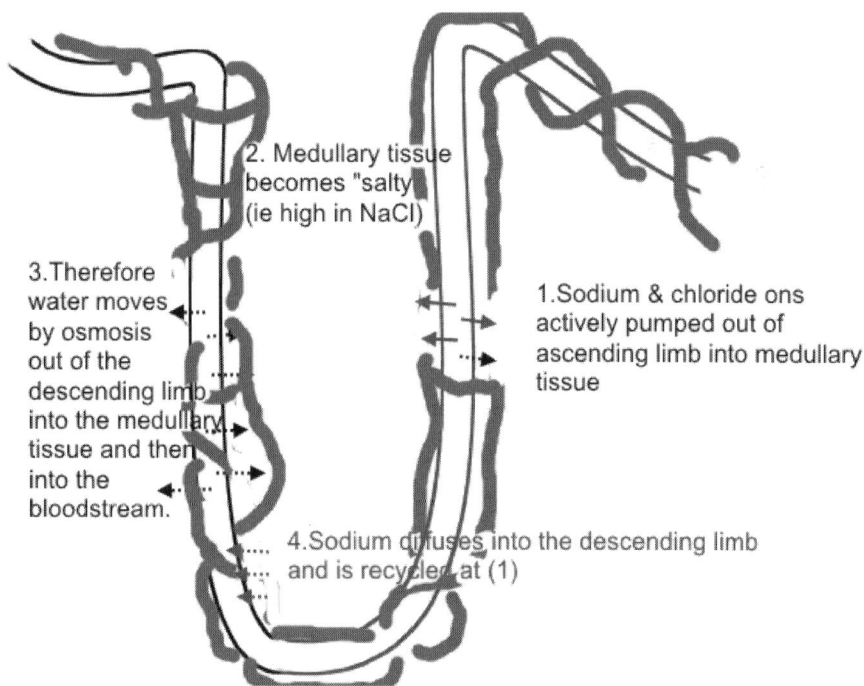

2. Medullary tissue becomes "salty" (ie high in NaCl)

3.Therefore water moves by osmosis out of the descending limb into the medullary tissue and then into the bloodstream.

1.Sodium & chloride ons actively pumped out of ascending limb into medullary tissue

4.Sodium diffuses into the descending limb and is recycled at (1)

In concentration terms this causes an increased solute concentration as you travel down the descending limb (due to water reabsorption). As one follows the fluid up the ascending limb, the concentrations of sodium and chloride ions reduce again due to active transport out of the tubule.

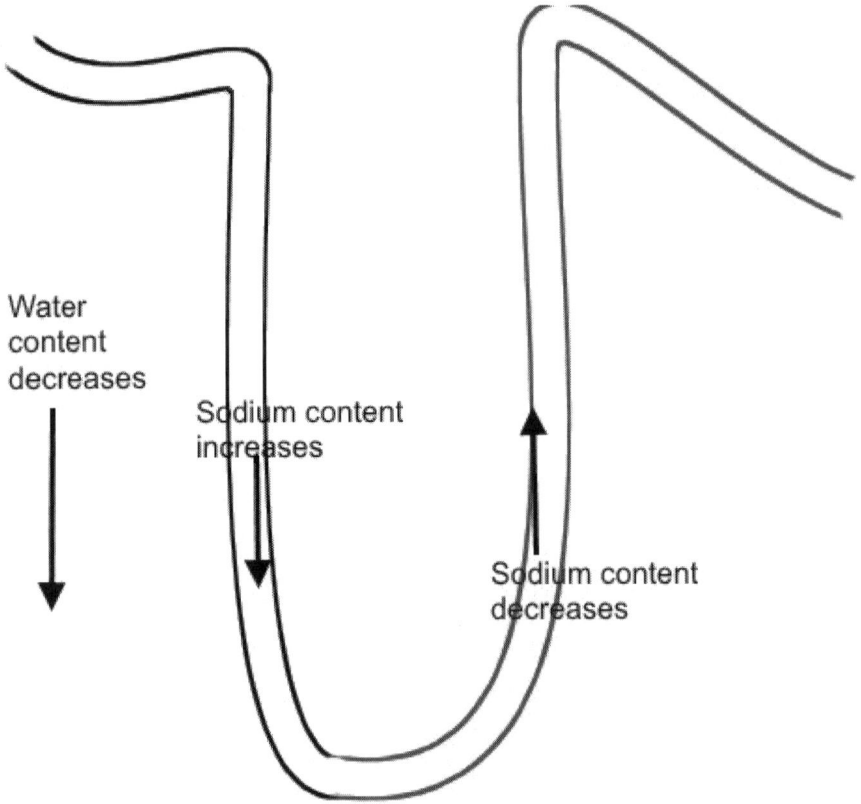

Water
content
decreases

Sodium content
increases

Sodium content
decreases

Nephron processes (4) – Variable water reabsorption in the collecting duct.

The majority of the collecting ducts are found in the medulla, leading into the renal pelvis. Thus the collecting ducts are also in the medullary tissue which is sodium chloride rich. The watery contents of the collecting duct therefore tend to move out of the duct into the medulla.

However the collecting duct walls are variably permeable to water allowing the body to maintain the correct water balance by more or less reabsorption into the blood.

How it happens

The hypothalamus was described in Book 2. This part of the brain monitors many of the body processes. It is connected to the pituitary gland. Apart from being a part of the brain, the hypothalamus can also manufacture hormones which are then secreted by the pituitary gland. When the body is becoming dehydrated, anti-diuretic hormone (ADH) is produced by the hypothalamus and released into the bloodstream by the pituitary.

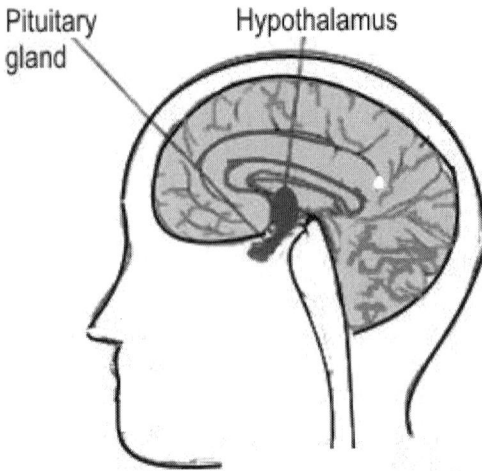

Pituitary gland   Hypothalamus

The inner face of the collecting duct walls is naturally impermeable to water. The cells making up the walls contain special vesicles which contain water channels. They are called "aquaporins".

ADH is carried to the kidneys and binds to ADH receptors located on the outer face of the collecting duct cell wall. (Actually the cell membranes of the cells making up the collecting duct wall).

This binding "repels" the vesicles to the inner face of the cells where they fuse, integrating the aquaporins with the membrane. The cells now become water permeable. Water flows into the medullary tissue and from thence into the bloodstream via the vasa recta.

The more ADH that is released, the more water channels are created and vice versa. This elegant system fine tunes the uptake of water. On a cold winters day, normally very little ADH will be secreted, therefore few water channels will be formed and little water reabsorbed. Consequently we pass larger quantities of dilute urine.

On a hot summer's day, we need to remain hydrated, therefore more ADH is released.

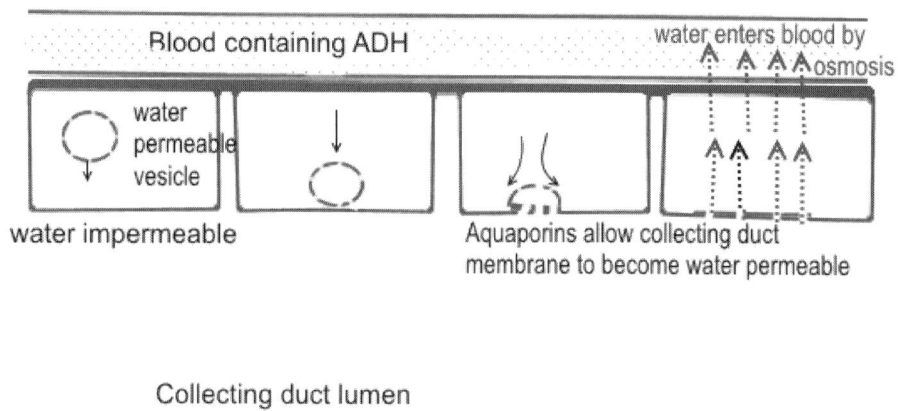

Blood containing ADH

water enters blood by osmosis

water permeable vesicle

water impermeable

Aquaporins allow collecting duct membrane to become water permeable

Collecting duct lumen

The kidneys and buffering

Buffering systems in the body help resist deviations from the optimum levels. The renal tubules are important in the buffering of a number of levels. This section outlines one example.

pH levels

Buffering is especially important for the pH in our bloodstream. Proteins-which include enzymes are vulnerable to extremes of pH and may cease to work, or even become denatured. As our body systems are enzyme mediated, the correct pH is a matter of life and death.

If blood plasma becomes acidified (i.e. the pH is reduced), **acidosis** results. Acidosis can result in confusion, headaches, abnormal blood pressure and heart rate. In serious cases it leads to coma and death.

Alternatively if the plasma becomes too alkaline metabolic OR respiratory **alkalosis/alkalaemia** results. Again, severe deviations lead to problems with nervous and brain function, as well as with the respiratory and cardiovascular systems. Alkalaemia, like acidosis, can prove fatal.

Two systems in particular operate to buffer blood pH. The breathing system increases breathing rate as pH falls, it slows breathing if pH swings too far in the other direction. This helps purge carbon dioxide from the system, or add carbon dioxide restoring pH towards neutrality. This is a quick response. However ongoing regulation is very effectively managed by the kidneys.

The renal tubules (and collecting duct) help with plasma pH by variously secreting positive hydrogen ions or absorbing hydrogencarbonate ions.

The DCT has various roles, including buffering the body against imbalances of potassium. Thus potassium can be either secreted into or reabsorbed from the glomerular filtrate variably in the DCT.

The kidneys and red blood cell regulation

The kidneys play a part in a number of other processes in the body. Specialised cells in the kidney interstitial tissue are constantly monitoring the levels of red blood cells (RBC) and oxygen in the blood passing through the kidneys.

If levels fall below a threshold, these kidney cells respond by releasing a hormone called erythropoietin (EPO) into the bloodstream.

The EPO is then carried in the bloodstream where it targets bone marrow stem cells. These stem cells are undifferentiated cells with the ability to develop into any type of blood cell; red, white or platelet.

The effect of EPO is to maximise production of RBC by the stem cells.

Once levels are satisfactory, the kidney cells adjust the EPO secretion downwards.

EPO is a thorny subject in athletic circles. It has often been illegally administered to athletes in order to boost RBC numbers and consequently give increased stamina.

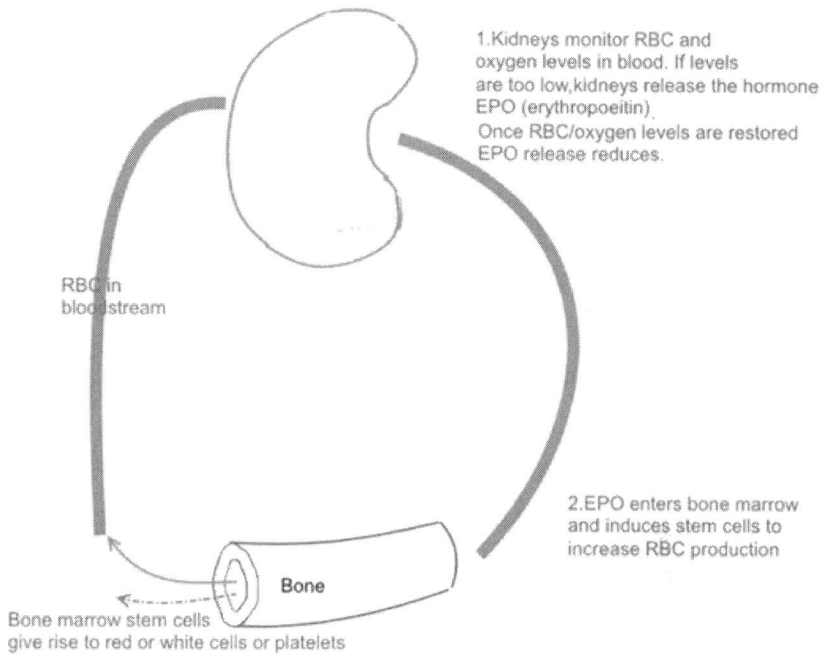

1.Kidneys monitor RBC and oxygen levels in blood. If levels are too low,kidneys release the hormone EPO (erythropoeitin).
Once RBC/oxygen levels are restored EPO release reduces.

RBC in bloodstream

2.EPO enters bone marrow and induces stem cells to increase RBC production

Bone

Bone marrow stem cells give rise to red or white cells or platelets

The kidneys and blood pressure

The kidneys also play a vital role in regulating blood pressure. They are part of the renin-angiotensin system. Very complex but here is a very brief outline.

How it happens.

Blood pressure (BP) is monitored within the kidneys. If BP falls, the kidneys release an enzyme called **renin** into the bloodstream. Renin converts a substance called angiotensin into an active form with the help of another enzyme ACE (released in the lungs). Angiotensin is produced by the liver. The active form of angiotensin (angiotensin 2) constricts blood vessels, thereby increasing BP. Thus ACE inhibitors may be of help to people with high BP. They reduce the amount of angiotensin 2 produced and thereby have a relaxing effect on blood vessels, reducing BP.

Acknowledgements:

P 6. Diagram of kidney layout: https://upload.wikimedia.org/wikipedia/commons/4/48/201405_ kidney.png [accessed 07/08/17]. Attribution DBCLS 統合TV [CC BY 4.0 (http://creativecommons.org/licenses/by/4.0)], via Wikimedia Commons

Further reading in the series

I hope you have enjoyed reading this book. Continue extending your confidence in biology with others in the series.

1. Basic Introductions to Biology – Cells tissues and circulation (in e-book format OR as a paperback)
2. Basic Introductions to Biology - Bacteria Viruses and Fungi
3. Basic Introductions to Biology - Disease and immunity: An introduction to defence, immunity and pharmacology
4. A basic introduction to chemistry
5. Quickfire Revision Questions for Biology (Book 1) available in e-book or paperback format.
6. Quickfire Revision Questions for Biology (Book 2-going deeper) available in e-book or paperback format.

Index

Printed in Poland
by Amazon Fulfillment
Poland Sp. z o.o., Wrocław